curious about

PRESIDENTS' DAY

BY AMY HOUTS

AMICUS LEARNING

What are you

CHAPTER ONE

A Birthday Celebration
PAGE **4**

CHAPTER TWO

The History of Presidents' Day
PAGE **10**

curious about?

CHAPTER THREE

Let's Celebrate!
PAGE **16**

Stay Curious! Learn More . . . 22
Glossary. 24
Index 24

Curious About is published by
Amicus Learning, an imprint of Amicus
P.O. Box 227, Mankato, MN 56002
www.amicuspublishing.us

Copyright © 2026 Amicus.
International copyright reserved in all countries.
No part of this book may be reproduced in any
form without written permission from the publisher.

Editor: Ana Brauer
Series Designer: Kathleen Petelinsek
Book Designer and Photo Researcher: Sara Hood

Library of Congress Cataloging-in-Publication Data
Names: Houts, Amy, 1957- author
Title: Curious about Presidents' Day / Amy Houts.
Description: Mankato, MN : Amicus Learning, 2026. |
Series: Curious about holidays | Includes bibliographical
references and index. | Audience: Ages 6–9 | Audience:
Grades 2–3 | Summary: "Discover the importance of
Presidents' Day! Learn about the holiday's history, significance,
and celebrations in this question-and-answer book for
elementary-aged readers. Includes table of contents, glossary,
further resources, and index"—Provided by publisher.
Identifiers: LCCN 2025014078 (print) | LCCN 2025014079
(ebook) | ISBN 9798892008501 library binding | ISBN
9798892009164 paperback | ISBN 9798892009829 ebook
Subjects: LCSH: Presidents' Day—Juvenile literature
Classification: LCC E176.8 .H68 2026 (print) | LCC E176.8
(ebook) | DDC 394.261—dc23/eng/20250509
LC record available at https://lccn.loc.gov/2025014078
LC ebook record available at https://lccn.loc.gov/2025014079

Photo Credits: Alamy Stock Photo/Everett Collection, 19, Historical Art Collection (HAC), 9, Peter Phipp/Travelshots.com, 20–21, Steve Skjold, 3, 17, Xinhua, 13, ZUMA Press, 18; Getty Images/Christophe Lehenaff, 8, Peter Unger, 2, 7; MapSVG/unknown, 17; Shutterstock/BOOCYS, cover, 1, CK Foto, 14–15, Roberto Galan, 16, Sean Pavone, 10; The Noun Project/InYoung Park, 22, 23; Juicy Fish, 22, 23; Wikimedia Commons/Adam Cuerden, 2, 11, George Peter Alexander Healy, 5, Gilbert Stuart, 4

Every effort has been made to contact copyright holders for material reproduced in this book. Any omissions will be rectified in subsequent printings if notice is given to the publisher.

Printed in United States of America

CHAPTER ONE

What is Presidents' Day?

A BIRTHDAY CELEBRATION

George Washington was president from 1789 until 1797.

It is a birthday **celebration**! Whose birthday? George Washington was the first president of the United States. Washington's Birthday is the **official** holiday. But President Abraham Lincoln's birthday is also in February. So, people called the holiday Presidents' Day. That name stuck.

Abraham Lincoln was president from 1861 until 1865.

Who celebrates Presidents' Day?

People in the United States. People of any age can celebrate. You can take part in Presidents' Day. The holiday doesn't just honor Washington and Lincoln. It honors all US presidents.

DID YOU KNOW?
Abraham Lincoln was the 16th president of the United States.

Mount Rushmore in South Dakota shows the faces of four presidents: Washington, Thomas Jefferson, Theodore Roosevelt, and Lincoln.

A BIRTHDAY CELEBRATION

A statue of Washington stands in New York City.

Why do people celebrate Presidents' Day?

Washington and Lincoln did great things for our country. They were great leaders. Washington led the army in the **Revolutionary War**. He helped start a new nation. Lincoln led the country during the **Civil War**. He helped free the **slaves**.

President Lincoln freed many enslaved people with the Emancipation Proclamation.

A BIRTHDAY CELEBRATION

CHAPTER 2

How long has Presidents' Day been celebrated?

Washington lived in the President's House in Philadelphia.

DID YOU KNOW? The White House didn't exist while Washington was president. He lived in Philadelphia and New York.

It has been celebrated since 1879. This is when it became a federal holiday. Washington's birthday is February 22. He became president in 1789. People celebrated his birthday while he was in office. Lincoln's birthday is February 12. People started celebrating it after he died in 1865.

President Lincoln was killed on April 14, 1865.

When is Presidents' Day?

It is the third Monday in February. It used to be on February 22. But people like having a three-day weekend. So, the government changed the date. In 1971, the federal holiday became the third Monday in February.

People visit the National Portrait Gallery in Washington, D.C., to learn about the US presidents.

THE HISTORY OF PRESIDENTS' DAY

13

THE HISTORY OF PRESIDENTS' DAY

George Washington lived at Mount Vernon in Virginia before he became president.

What do people do for Presidents' Day?

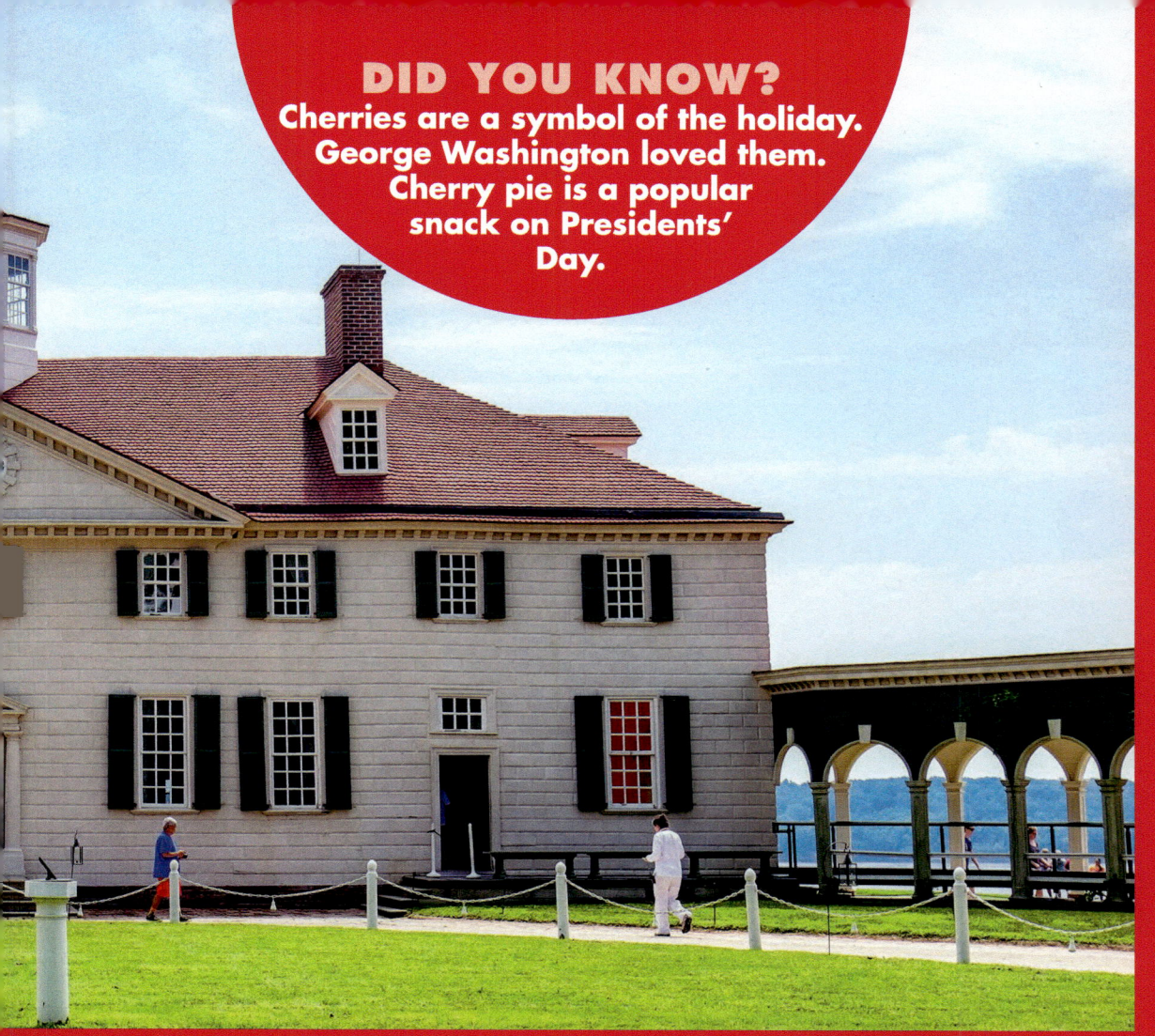

DID YOU KNOW?
Cherries are a symbol of the holiday. George Washington loved them. Cherry pie is a popular snack on Presidents' Day.

THE HISTORY OF PRESIDENTS' DAY

You might have the day off from school. Some people don't have to work. Many people learn about the presidents. They might visit Washington's home in Mount Vernon, Virginia. Others go to Lincoln's home in Springfield, Illinois. Some people watch sports or go shopping.

CHAPTER THREE

How do people celebrate Presidents' Day?

A man dresses as George Washington in a Presidents' Day parade.

Presidents' Day isn't like other holidays. People don't get together with family. But some states have yearly celebrations. Virginia has parties all month! It has the biggest parade, too. The George Washington Birthday Parade is a yearly event.

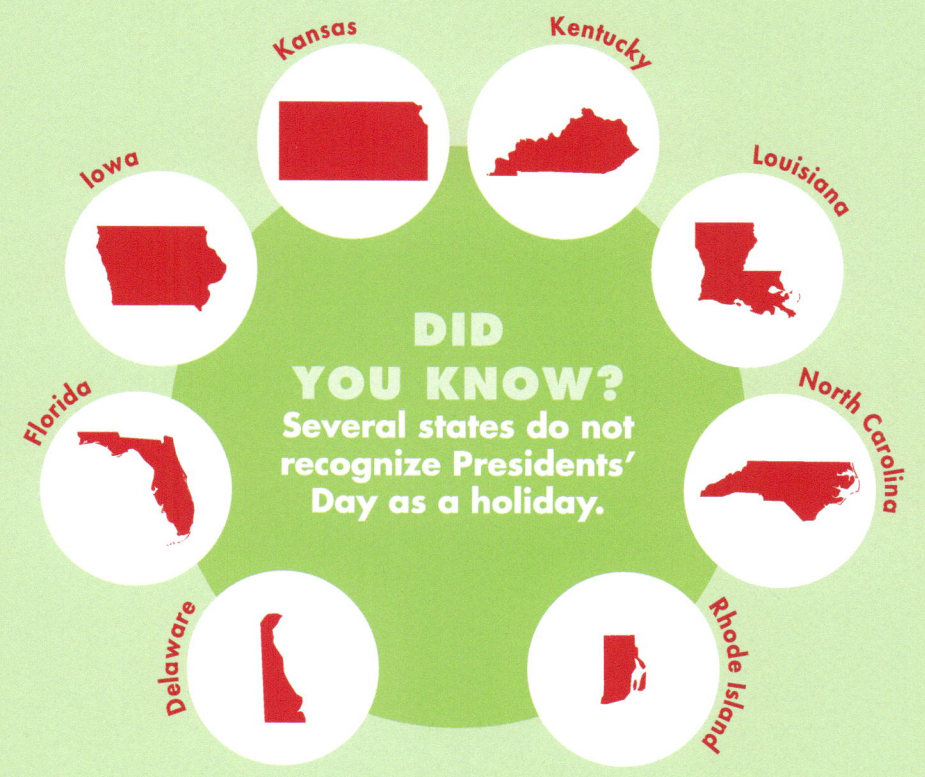

Some kids give reports about George Washington on Presidents' Day.

DID YOU KNOW? Several states do not recognize Presidents' Day as a holiday.

Kansas · Kentucky · Louisiana · North Carolina · Rhode Island · Delaware · Florida · Iowa

LET'S CELEBRATE!

Who else is celebrated on Presidents' Day?

LET'S CELEBRATE!

Daisy Gatson Bates stood up for equal rights during the Civil Rights Movement.

Arkansas celebrates a civil rights leader. Her name is Daisy Gatson Bates. She helped children of different races go to school together. So, Arkansas has two names for this holiday. It's also called Daisy Gatson Bates Day.

In 1957, Daisy Gatson Bates (top row, second from right) helped the Little Rock Nine go to a white school in Arkansas.

DID YOU KNOW?
Mexico celebrates their former president Benito Juarez on the third Monday of March.

Do other countries honor their presidents?

People in the United Kingdom celebrate the king's birthday every June.

Yes, other countries honor their presidents. They might celebrate on their birthday. But some countries don't have a president. They have other leaders. These leaders have other titles like king or queen. Many countries celebrate their leaders with parades and parties.

STAY CURIOUS!

ASK MORE QUESTIONS

What are some symbols of Presidents' Day?

How did President Lincoln free the slaves?

Try a BIG QUESTION: What good things did other presidents do?

SEARCH FOR ANSWERS

Search the library catalog or the Internet.
A librarian, teacher, or parent can help you.

Using Keywords
Find the looking glass.

Keywords are the most important words in your question.

?

If you want to know about:
- symbols for Presidents' Day, type: PRESIDENTS' DAY SYMBOLS
- how Lincoln helped free slaves, type: EMANCIPATION PROCLAMATION